Strategic Studies Institute
and
U.S. Army War College Press

SOLDIERS OF MISFORTUNE?

Thomas R. Mockaitis

May 2014

*****

Comments pertaining to this report are invited and should be forwarded to: Director, Strategic Studies Institute and U.S. Army War College Press, U.S. Army War College, 47 Ashburn Drive, Carlisle, PA 17013-5010.

*****

This manuscript was funded by the U.S. Army War College External Research Associates Program. Information on this program is available on our website, *www.StrategicStudies Institute.army.mil*, at the Opportunities tab.

*****

The Strategic Studies Institute and U.S. Army War College Press publishes a monthly email newsletter to update the national security community on the research of our analysts, recent and forthcoming publications, and upcoming conferences sponsored by the Institute. Each newsletter also provides a strategic commentary by one of our research analysts. If you are interested in receiving this newsletter, please subscribe on the SSI website at *www.StrategicStudiesInstitute.army.mil/newsletter*.

FOREWORD

The long counterinsurgency campaigns in Iraq and Afghanistan have made two facts abundantly clear about military contractors: 1) The U.S. Army has become dependent upon them; and, 2) They frequently create problems for, and sometimes actually interfere with, accomplishing the mission. In order to free up Soldiers for their core task of fighting and winning the nation's wars, the U.S. Government began in the 1980s to hire private companies to provide services previously handled by the military itself. Contractors gradually took over building bases, running mess halls, and doing laundry for U.S. troops at home and abroad. Providing such logistics support allowed a smaller land force to do as much as a large one had previously done. Logistics contractors also provided a surge capacity. They could be hired for a mission and let go once the mission was completed. The military also found it expedient to outsource maintenance of new high-tech weapons systems rather than assume the cost of developing and maintaining its own support capability.

Other than occasional cases of waste, fraud, and abuse, logistics and technical support contractors caused no serious problems and, indeed, were a valuable force multiplier. That situation changed dramatically with the 2003 invasion of Iraq. To bolster its military mission in the face of a growing insurgency, the George W. Bush administration deployed a small army of armed security personnel employed by private military security contractors (PMSCs). PMSCs provided personnel security details, convoy escorts, and facilities guards for the Departments of Defense and State, the U.S. Agency for International Development, and a host of other agencies and departments. Operating in a legal vacuum, these contractors were armed like Soldiers but dressed like civilians. In carrying out their jobs, they often acted in a heavy-handed manner toward Iraqi civilians and got involved in several escalation-of-force incidents. The Army had similar problems with contractors in Afghanistan. These problems called into question the wisdom of using PMSCs in contingency operations.

This monograph examines the role of security contractors in Iraq and Afghanistan. From analysis of these two missions, it draws broad lessons from which it derives concrete recommendations to improve the conduct of further missions. Rather than do away with PMSCs altogether, the author recommends limiting their roles, providing better oversight of their activities, and improving legal accountability for their wrong doing. This monograph will be of interest to Soldiers and policymakers engaged in the difficult task of planning and conducting contingency operations.

DOUGLAS C. LOVELACE, JR.
Director
Strategic Studies Institute and
    U.S. Army War College Press

ABOUT THE AUTHOR

THOMAS R. MOCKAITIS is a professor of history at DePaul University. He team-teaches terrorism and counterterrorism courses internationally with other experts through the Center for Civil-Military Relations at the Naval Post-Graduate School. He was the 2004 Eisenhower Chair at the Royal Military Academy of the Netherlands. He has also lectured at the North Atlantic Treaty Organization School, the U.S. Marine Corps Command and Staff College, and the Canadian Forces Staff College. He has presented papers at the Pearson Peacekeeping Center (Canada), the Royal Military Academy Sandhurst (UK), and the Austrian National Defense Academy. A frequent media commentator on terrorism and security matters, Dr. Mockaitis has appeared on Public Television, National Public Radio, BBC World News, all major Chicago TV stations, and various local radio programs. He appears regularly as a terrorism expert for WGN-TV News. He is the 2008 recipient of the DePaul Liberal Arts and Sciences Cortelyou-Lowery Award for Excellence in Teaching, Scholarship, and Service. Dr. Mockaitis is the author of *Avoiding the Slippery Slope: Mounting Interventions* (Carlisle, PA: Strategic Studies Institute, U.S. Army War College, 2013), *The Iraq War: A Documentary and Reference Guide* (Santa Barbara, CA: ABC-Clio/Greenwood, 2012), *Osama bin Laden: A Biography* (Westport, CT: Greenwood, 2010), *Iraq and the Challenge of Counterinsurgency* (Westport, CT: Praeger, 2008), *The "New" Terrorism: Myths and Reality* (Westport, CT: Praeger, 2007), *The Iraq War: Learning from the Past, Adapting to the Present, and Preparing for the Future* (Carlisle, PA: Strategic Studies Institute, U.S. Army War College, 2007), *Peacekeeping and Intrastate*

Conflict: the Sword or the Olive Branch? (Westport, CT: Praeger, 1999), *British Counterinsurgency in the Post-Imperial Era* (Manchester, UK: University of Manchester Press, 1995), and *British Counterinsurgency: 1919-1960* (London, UK: Macmillan, 1990). He co-edited *Grand Strategy and the War on Terrorism* with Paul Rich, (London, UK: Frank Cass, 2003) and *The Future of Peace Operations: Old Challenges for a New Century* with Erwin Schmidl (a special issue of *Small Wars and Insurgencies*, London, UK: Taylor and Francis, 2004). He is an editor of *Small Wars and Insurgencies* and has also published numerous articles on unconventional conflict. His most recent work, an encyclopedia of the Iraq War, was published by ABC-Clio/Greenwood in August 2013. Dr. Mockaitis earned his B.A. in European history from Allegheny College, and his M.A. and Ph.D. in modern British and Irish history from the University of Wisconsin-Madison.

SUMMARY

Private contractors have become an essential but highly problematic element in the U.S. military's total force structure. The Army in particular relies heavily on contractors to perform duties that free up Soldiers for combat roles. The vast majority of these civilian employees provide logistical and technical support. They build facilities, do laundry, and staff dining halls on U.S. bases at home and abroad. While some of these contractors have been involved in issues of waste, fraud, and abuse, these issues do not have a significant effect on the conduct of contingency operations, especially counterinsurgency (COIN) campaigns.

The same cannot be said of a small subset of military contractors known as private military security contractors (PMSCs). PMSCs provide armed security personnel to support contingency operations abroad. They provide heavily armed personal security details for the Department of Defense (DoD), the Department of State (DoS), the U.S. Agency for International Development (USAID), construction contractors, nongovernmental and international organizations (NGOs and IOs), and even private individuals. They also supply static security guards for bases and other facilities, and escort supply convoys in conflict zones. These activities have embroiled them in escalation-of-force and other incidents that have undermined mission goals and objectives. Reigning in security contractors thus presents a major challenge for the U.S. Government in general and the Army in particular.

This monograph examines the role of PMSCs in Iraq and Afghanistan in order to derive general lessons on employment of security contractors in future contingency operations, particularly COIN campaigns.

Three broad questions underlie this analysis. First, what tasks can be safely outsourced to private companies? Second, how should the government manage contractors in conflict zones? Closely related to the issue of oversight is the third analytical question: Under what laws should PMSCs be held legally accountable for their actions? Based on these questions, the author identifies areas in which armed contractors seem to create the most problems. Convoy escorts and personal security details have frequently become involved in escalation-of-force incidents. He also raises serious concerns about employment of security guards from the local population and discusses the several legal frameworks under which all civilian security contractors might fall.

Based upon analysis of the two campaigns using the three analytical questions, the author identifies important lessons and makes specific recommendations based upon these lessons. First, contractor roles and tasks should be assigned based not upon whether their duties would be inherently governmental (the current standard for restricting such activities to Soldiers), but upon whether those duties are likely to bring them into violent contact with local people. Second, at the very least, legal accountability should be written into the PMSC contract, and, at best, Congress should pass laws specifically governing the behavior of armed contractors. Third, interagency cooperation among all those employing PMSC personnel must be strengthened. Fourth, oversight of contractors must be improved. Fifth, employment of locals by government contractors should be restricted to nonsecurity activities, especially in environments in which those employees might have divided loyalties. Sixth, the DoD should consider the degree to which outsourcing logistics activities increases an expeditionary force's footprint and thus its need for security personnel. Seventh, Congress should take action to prevent use by the executive branch of security contracts as "workarounds," a means to conduct controversial activities without answering to the legislative branch. The monograph concludes with discussion of the implications these recommendations have for U.S. Landpower development.

SOLDIERS OF MISFORTUNE?

INTRODUCTION

On March 31, 2004, a convoy carrying kitchen equipment to a U.S. military base entered the Iraqi city of Fallujah. The four American security guards escorting it had considered skirting the town, but decided that conditions were safe enough for them to go through it and save time. They could not have been more wrong. Foot and automobile traffic brought the vehicles to a standstill after which they came under heavy machine gun and rifle fire. The carefully laid ambush quickly dispatched all four men. The crowd mutilated their bodies, lit them on fire, and hung the charred remains from a bridge where they would be seen on television screens around the world.[1]

For most American viewers, the Fallujah ambush provided a rude awakening to the deteriorating situation in Iraq, but it also introduced them to a new aspect of modern warfare. The four dead guards were not U.S. military personnel, but employees of Blackwater USA, a private company few had heard of before the killings thrust it onto the front page. This would not be the last time the company found itself embroiled in controversy during the Iraq War. On Christmas Eve 2006, another Blackwater employee left a party in the Green Zone drunk and got into an altercation with an Iraqi security guard who was protecting Iraqi Vice President Adil Abdul-Mahdi. The American shot the Iraqi guard dead and fled the scene; Blackwater quickly got its employee out of the country to avoid legal and political repercussions.[2]

Worse was yet to come. Around noon on September 16, 2007, a convoy escorted by Blackwater security

1

guards entered Nisour Square in Baghdad. After inexplicably making a U-turn and heading the wrong way down a one-way street (perhaps because they heard an explosion in the distance), the guards opened fire on a car they claimed had come too close to their convoy, a claim virtually all observers of the tragedy dispute. After stopping the car, the guards continued to fire, killing 14 Iraqi civilians and wounding 20 others.[3] A Federal Bureau of Investigation (FBI) investigation found no evidence that anyone had fired at the convoy and noted that some guards mistook fire by their comrades as coming from Iraqis. The investigation also found the killing of the 14 victims unjustified.[4]

Blackwater thus became emblematic of a new and, according to many observers, pernicious phenomenon in U.S. military operations: the outsourcing to private companies of key security activities previously done by Soldiers. ArmorGroup, Custer Battles, Triple Canopy, and a host of other hitherto unknown corporate entities took on duties once performed by servicemen and women. These companies made news only when they engaged in wrong-doing, so the American public formed a profoundly negative impression of them. Their operatives have been described as "mercenaries," "hired guns," "cowboys," and "rogue operatives" with a "license to kill."[5]

Unfortunately, these strong impressions impede objective analysis of a very complex phenomenon. Contractors play an essential, perhaps even indispensible, role in support of U.S. military operations. Like them or not, they are here to stay. The challenge is to use them effectively so that they enhance rather than diminish the effectiveness of U.S. forces responding to threats across the conflict spectrum. Improvement in the employment and oversight of contractor use should be based upon assessment of PMSC performance in the most recent contingency operations, Iraq and Afghanistan, and lessons learned from those operations.

This monograph undertakes such an assessment, focusing on this particular variety of contractor in a specific type of situation. It examines the advantages and disadvantages of using PMSCs in counterinsurgency (COIN) campaigns. These companies provide armed personnel who engage in security tasks likely to bring them into violent conflict with insurgents and/or local civilians. This monograph does not consider the far less controversial role of contractors providing logistics and technical support, except to the degree that those activities require greater numbers of security personnel, which, in turn, increases the risk of escalation-of-force and other incidents. It also leaves aside the challenging issues of waste, fraud, and abuse in the letting and oversight of all contracts, not because these issues are unimportant, but because they have less direct effect on COIN operations than do the security activities of PMSCs. No-bid contracts and poor oversight of companies providing logistics support waste money; poor management of private security guards costs lives and alienates local people, often driving them into the arms of the insurgents.

Three broad questions underlie this analysis of PMSCs in COIN campaigns. First: What tasks can be safely outsourced to private companies? The government prohibits hiring civilians to perform "inherently governmental functions," which it defines as activities "so intimately related to the public interest as to require performance by Federal Government employees."[6] The restriction precludes contractors from direct involvement in combat operations, but allows them to participate in a broad range of activities that could bring them into violent conflict with insurgents and/or local civilians. Roles and missions of civilian contractors thus require more precise definition. The second analytical question is: How should the government manage contractors in conflict zones? PMSCs serve a plethora of organizations and entities. In addition to the Department of Defense (DoD), the Department of State (DoS) and the U.S. Agency for International Development (USAID) employ private security personnel as do nongovernmental and international organizations (NGOs and IOs), as well as private individuals such as journalists. Contractors engaged in nonsecurity tasks such as construction also subcontract PMSCs, who protect the primary contractor's worksites, supply convoys, and personnel. Numerous employers with different objectives create serious oversight problems as no single entity manages PMSCs within an operational area. Closely related to the issue of oversight is the third analytical question: To whom should PMSCs be held legally accountable for their actions? In Iraq and Afghanistan, PMSCs have operated in a legal limbo, answerable neither to local nor to U.S. law. Efforts to remedy this problem have met with limited success.

The organization of this monograph supports its objectives. After delineating the nature of PMSCs and discussing the tasks they perform, it moves to consideration of their roles in the Iraq and Afghan wars, the problems they encountered, and efforts to address those difficulties. The monograph then derives lessons from these campaigns and makes recommendations based upon these lessons. It concludes with discussion of the implications these recommendations have for U.S. Army land forces development.

CONTRACTORS AND THE U.S. MILITARY

Contrary to popular perceptions, contracting out support services for the U.S. military is not new. The Army has long relied on private contractors to provide supplies and perform some limited duties to free up service personnel for combat roles. Since the mid-1980s, however, use of contractors has steadily increased. President Ronald Reagan entered office committed to reducing the cost of government amid a climate of opinion that believed the private sector performed more efficiently than the public.[7] This mentality affected the Pentagon as well as other departments and agencies. In 1985, the Army established its first Logistics Civil Augmentation Program (LOGCAP) to plan for use of contractors in support of regular and reserve forces during crises and contingency operations.[8] At the time, no one imagined that contingency operations would involve anything like the sustained COIN campaigns of Iraq and Afghanistan.

The 1990s saw military contracting expand dramatically. This growth resulted from a number of factors. The decade saw an acceleration of what has been dubbed "the privatization revolution," a trend in which the United States and the United Kingdom (UK) outsourced more and more government work to the private sector.[9] Receiving the lion's share of the federal budget, the DoD was a prime candidate for outsourcing. Two other factors accelerated the trend toward increased use of contractors. First, the end of the Cold War created public demand for a peace dividend with a concomitant reduction in the size of U.S. forces. Unfortunately, the United States cut defense spending without shedding security commitments.

Peace-building missions to Somalia, Bosnia, and Kosovo required major U.S. troop deployments. Hiring contractors like Kellogg, Brown and Root (a subsidiary of Halliburton Corporation) to build camps and run food service facilities proved cost effective (although issues of waste, fraud, and abuse did arise). During the mission to Bosnia, for example, contracted services included "[building] troop housing and facilities, food service operations, laundry operations, base camp and equipment maintenance, and cargo handling throughout the area of operations."[10] Technology was the second factor that accelerated the privatization trend. Increasingly complex weapons systems required skilled maintenance professionals that the military did not have. Hiring the very companies who produced the new weapons to provide this expertise made economic sense.

THE UNIQUE NATURE OF
PRIVATE MILITARY SECURITY CONTRACTORS

Logistics and technical support contractors make up the bulk of those employed in support of military operations, but they are not the primary source of contractor controversy. That dubious distinction belongs to a particular subset of contractors known as PMSCs. These companies actually employ armed personnel to provide physical security to their clients. In Iraq and Afghanistan, physical security has included escorting convoys, guarding bases and other facilities, and protecting personnel. All of these tasks require PMSC personnel to be armed (sometimes quite heavily) and carry the risk that these employees will come into violent contact with insurgents and/or civilians. The DoD, DoS, and USAID hire private security personnel, as do NGOs and IOs. Government contractors performing nonsecurity tasks such as construction may also subcontract with PMSCs to guard work sites and provide personnel security. While PMSCs are not new, their role in U.S. COIN operations certainly is. Prior to Iraq, the U.S. military and other government entities did not rely heavily on PMSCs in war zones.

Because of the controversy surrounding both groups and the tendency to conflate them in the popular imagination, a clear distinction must be made between mercenaries and PMSCs. The 1977 Protocol of the 1949 Geneva Convention defines a mercenary as any person who:

> a. is specially recruited locally or abroad in order to fight in an armed conflict;
>
> b. does, in fact, take a direct part in the hostilities;
>
> c. is motivated to take part in the hostilities essentially by the desire for private gain and, in fact, is promised, by or on behalf of a party to the conflict, material compensation substantially in excess of that promised or paid to combatants of similar ranks and functions in the armed forces of that party;
>
> d. is neither a national of a party to the conflict nor a resident of territory controlled by a party to the conflict;
>
> e. is not a member of the armed forces of a party to the conflict; and,
>
> f. has not been sent by a state which is not a party to the conflict on official duty as a member of its armed forces.[11]

In 1989, the United Nations (UN) expanded the definition of a mercenary to include anyone who is specially recruited locally or abroad for the purpose of participating in a concerted act of violence aimed at: 1) overthrowing a government or otherwise undermining the constitutional order of a state; or, 2) undermining the territorial integrity of a state.[12]

PMSCs have some, but not all, of the characteristics of mercenaries. They clearly work for profit and are not members of the regular armed forces, but they are usually employed by a state. Whether they actually engage in combat has been the subject of much debate. The Geneva Protocol and the UN resolution were not written with contemporary PMSCs in mind. These agreements were meant to address the plague of mercenaries that descended upon Africa during the era of decolonization following World War II. They have proven wholly inadequate in addressing the problems of PMSCs in the 21st century.

IRAQ AND THE CONTRACTOR SURGE

Despite their increased use in contingency operations during the 1990s, military contractors did not create controversy until Operation IRAQI FREEDOM. This controversy arose predominantly from the widespread use of PMSCs and the problems caused by their employees. The dramatic increase in government contractors in general, and PMSCs in particular, resulted from the contrast between the war the Pentagon expected to fight in Iraq and the one it actually got. Determined to avoid what it had derisively dubbed "nation building," the administration of President George W. Bush prepared for a short, decisive campaign. Secretary of Defense Donald Rumsfeld kept the invasion force as small as possible and delayed creation of the Office of Humanitarian Aid, the body tasked with post-war reconstruction.[13] Ignoring any voice that raised the prospect of civil strife, the Pentagon planned to invade Iraq, hand it over to an interim government, and withdraw troops as soon as possible.[14] They failed to anticipate the total collapse of the Iraqi state and were thus unprepared for the law and order role they needed to perform. Widespread looting wrecked an already fragile infrastructure. Unemployment soared and unrest spread as foreign mujahedeen flooded into the country. Terrorism and intercommunal violence ensued. By the fall of 2003, the U.S.-led mission faced a full-blown insurgency.

With too few troops on the ground, the administration faced a difficult choice. To fill the security gap with uniformed military personnel would have required a significant call-up of Reserve and National Guard units, which might well have met with popular opposition, especially since the President had promised a short war.[15] With campaigning for the 2004 presidential election about to begin, the political cost of deploying more combat troops with a corresponding increase in casualties was deemed too high. The administration chose to surge contractors rather than Soldiers. Until they became embroiled in controversy, contractors drew little public attention and avoided both congressional oversight and an embarrassing policy debate on the war in Iraq.[16] Contractor deaths were usually not reported and so did not produce the same reaction from the public as did military casualties. Surging contractors was a cost-saving measure, but "the cost savings were political in nature."[17] One study succinctly described the thinking in Washington:

> Using contractors speeds policy response but limits input into the policy process. As the insurgency grew in Iraq, for example, the United States mobilized 150,000

to 170,000 private forces to support the mission there, all with little or no congressional or public knowledge– let alone consent. President Bush was not required to appeal to Congress or the public for these additional forces, which doubled the U.S. presence in Iraq.[18]

The difficulty President Bush had in persuading Congress and the country to surge 30,000 additional troops to Iraq in 2007 suggests he might have encountered much more resistance if he had asked to send an additional 150,000 troops in 2004.[19] The terms of some contracts protected their holders from the Freedom of Information Act, and even when they did not, the government refused to release some information about them.[20]

The number of contractors in Iraq increased dramatically over the next few years, reaching a high of 190,000 by early-2008.[21] The amount paid to contractors in Iraq rose from approximately $5 billion in 2003 to more than $10 billion in 2004 and more than $15 billion in 2005. Only a small percentage of contractors performed security duties, but their numbers also increased dramatically. The number of armed contractors doubled between 2003 and 2004, increasing from 10,000 to 20,000, and peaked at 30,000 in 2007.[22] Some sources put the number of private security personnel much higher. The Director of the Private Security Association of Iraq estimated that 181 PMSCs employed 48,000 people in Iraq in 2007.[23]

Private security personnel worked for a variety of actors, adding to the complexity of managing them. The DoD and DoS employed the largest number, followed by USAID. By 2008, the height of PMSC presence in Iraq, the DoD was employing 7,000 private security personnel and the DoS 3,000.[24] USAID employed 3,500 contractors but did not provide data on their function.[25] Assuming that their needs were roughly analogous to those of the DoS, which used approximately 40 percent of its contractors for security,[26] USAID employed about 1,800 security contractors. However, since USAID provides data only on prime contractors, this number does not include PMSCs subcontracted by USAID contractors engaged in relief and reconstruction projects, many of which required security guards for their work sites and armed escorts for their supply convoys, as well as protection for personnel.[27] The remaining U.S. Government agencies employing contractors included "the Departments of Agriculture, Commerce, Health and Human Services, the Interior, Justice, Transportation, and the Treasury, as well as the Broadcasting Board of Governors and the General Services Administration."[28] The mere fact that so many departments and agencies cannot (or will not) provide complete, accurate data on the number of contractors they employed in Iraq disaggregated by function is deeply troubling and indicative of more serious oversight problems. Further complicating the security sector situation was the host of PMSC personnel employed by NGOs journalists, and virtually everyone else who worked in Iraq.

The diverse backgrounds and nationalities of contractors added to the challenge of managing them effectively. A 2005 Public Broadcasting System (PBS) *Frontline* story provided a useful profile of contractors in Iraq at the time, breaking down their numbers by function:

- 50,000 support/logistics contractors. These are civilians hired by companies KBR [Kellogg, Brown and Root], the Halliburton subsidiary, which holds the military's logistical support contract

(LOGCAP). For example, these contractors work as weathermen, cooks, carpenters, and mechanics. Most are from the developing world; the majority are Filipino.

- 20,000 non-Iraqi security contractors. Of these, 5,000-6,000 are British, American, South African, Russian, or European; another 12,000 are from such developing countries as Fiji, Colombia, Sri Lanka, and India.
- 15,000 Iraqi security contractors. Most of these were hired, mainly by the British security firm Erinys, to guard Iraq's oil infrastructure.
- 40,000-70,000 reconstruction contractors. Some are Iraqi, but most are from the United States and dozens of other countries, and are employed by companies such as General Electric, Bechtel, Parsons, KBR, Fluor, and Perini.[29]

Employing local Iraqis enmeshed in the complex network of family, tribe, clan, ethnic, and religious groups that often mistrusted and sometimes fought with one another proved especially problematic.

CONTRACTORS AND CONTROVERSY

Many of the 30,000 or so PMSC personnel in Iraq performed their duties admirably and without serious incident. Those who got into trouble, however, did serious damage to the COIN effort being mounted by coalition forces. As with so much contractor activity, precise data on incidents is hard to find, especially since employees were reporting to their own companies, which had a vested interest in downplaying the number and seriousness of abuses. Other than the handful of prominent incidents identified at the beginning of this monograph, very few cases have received much attention. Nonetheless, some data has been released, which, although understated, still presents a disturbing picture of what went on in Iraq. Numerous eyewitness accounts put flesh on the bare bones of this data. Together they paint a very disturbing picture of contractor behavior in Iraq.

In 2008, journalist Jonathan Cook filed a Freedom of Information Act with the DoS requesting incident reports for PMSCs employed by the DoS for the period 2005-07. The request yielded 4,500 pages of documents recording 600 incidents in which a contractor discharged a weapon in Iraq.[30] Most of the reported incidents (65 percent) involved contractors firing at vehicles which they claimed posed a threat to the convoy or motorcade they were escorting; the documents record 10 Iraqi fatalities.[31] Reports varied in length, there is no record of a follow-up investigation in 95 percent of the cases, and only 5 cases were referred to the Justice Department for possible prosecution.[32] The documents also contain evidence of deliberate falsification by contractors. One report indicated that the Iraqi vehicle contractors fired upon was on a "lookout list" of vehicles previously identified as suspicious. However, one guard reported that claiming targeted vehicles were on the list was "simply standard practice when reporting a shooting incident, per Blackwater management."[33]

The fragmentary nature of the data makes it very difficult to determine how frequently such incidents occurred, never mind ascertaining in how many cases firing was justified. The DoS documents indicate that shooting incidents occurred in 2 percent of the 5,648 cases in which armed security contractors escorted motorcades, a figure corroborated by congressional testimony.[34] However, the documents cover only a 2-year period and report only those incidents involving DoS contractors. Add to that the fact that government departments and agencies relied on PMSCs to self-report incidents, and it becomes evident that a strong inferential case can be made that far more incidents occurred than were ever reported. A survey of military and DoS personnel by the Rand Corporation also points to a higher incidence of contractor misconduct than official records indicate. The Rand study found that "in the experience of military personnel, incidents in which armed contractors behaved in an unnecessarily threatening, arrogant, or belligerent way in Iraq were not entirely uncommon." The report stressed that:

> although a majority of surveyed personnel had never witnessed an event of this sort, the number of respondents with experience interacting with armed contractors who reported having sometimes observed such behavior (20 percent) is a substantial figure.[35]

Further evidence of under-reporting comes from the Congressional Memorandum on the Nisour Square Shootings. Using internal company documents as well as DoS reports, the investigating committee found that from January 1, 2005, to October 2007, Blackwater personnel were involved in 195 escalation-of-force incidents, an average of 1.4 shootings per week, some of which were not previously reported to the DoS.[36] Incidents of opening fire may, in fact, have been much greater. According to one Blackwater guard, his 20-man team opened fire "4-5 times a week," much more frequently than the congressional memo indicates.[37] Investigators found evidence of DoS officials encouraging Blackwater to pay cash settlements to families of Iraqis killed by its operatives to resolve the incidents quickly and quietly.[38] The memo offered a damning conclusion about the company's attitude toward use of force:

> The Blackwater and State Department Records reveal that Blackwater's use of force in Iraq is frequent and extensive, resulting in significant casualties and property damage. Blackwater is legally and contractually bound to engage only in defensive use of force to prevent 'imminent and grave danger' to themselves or others. In practice, however, the vast majority of Blackwater weapons discharges [84 percent] are preemptive, with Blackwater forces firing first at a vehicle or suspicious individual prior to receiving any fire.[39]

Blackwater was the worst, but by no means the only, offender. The memo found evidence of escalation of force incidents involving DynCorp and Triple Canopy.

Eyewitness accounts and the statements of officers and contractors themselves fill out this disturbing statistical picture of PMSC behavior in Iraq. U.S. Commanders have commented that Blackwater security guards "have very quick trigger fingers," "shoot first and ask questions later," and "act like cowboys."[40] Brigadier General Karl Horst, Deputy Commander of the Third Infantry Division, was scathingly critical of contractor behavior during his July 2005 tour. "These guys run loose in this country and do stupid stuff. . . ," he complained. "They shoot people, and someone else has to deal with the aftermath."[41] He did not confine his criticism to Blackwater. He further noted that contractors employed by Zapata:

> were doing what we call 'clearing by fire' . . . They were shooting everything they see. They blew through here and they shot at our guys and they just kept going. No one was shooting back.[42]

Another diplomat used similar language to describe what he observed: Blackwater guards "behave like Iraq is the Wild West and Iraqis are like 'Injuns,' to be treated any way they like," he observed. "They're better-armed and -armored than the military, but they don't have to follow military rules, and that makes them dangerous."[43]

The Coalition Provisional Authority (CPA) headed by L. Paul ("Jerry") Bremer did much to encourage what some have called a "culture of impunity."[44] In June 2003, Bremer issued CPA General Order No. 17:

> 1. Coalition contractors and their sub-contractors, as well as their employees not normally resident in Iraq, shall not be subject to Iraqi laws or regulations in matters relating to the terms and conditions of their contracts in relation to the Coalition Forces or the CPA. Coalition contractors and sub-contractors other than contractors and sub-contractors normally resident in Iraq shall not be subject to Iraqi laws or regulations with respect to licensing and registration of employees, businesses and corporations in relation to such contracts.

> 2. Coalition contractors and their sub-contractors as well as their employees not normally resident in Iraq, shall be immune from Iraqi Legal Process with respect to acts performed by them within their official activities pursuant to the terms and conditions of a contract between a contractor and Coalition Forces or the CPA and any sub-contract thereto.[45]

Bremer clearly intended to protect coalition personnel from malicious prosecution in Iraqi courts, but his order overlooked an important point. At that time, the Uniform Code of Military Justice governing the behavior of uniformed members of the armed services did not apply to contractors. *U.S. Army Field Manual 3-100.21* made this limitation explicitly clear:

> Duties of contractors are established solely by the terms of their contract—they are not subject to Army regulations or the Uniform Code of Military Justice (UCMJ) (except during a declared war).[46]

In theory, contractors could be held accountable under U.S. law, but prosecuting them in American courts has proven very difficult even when there was the political will to do so. PMSC personnel thus operated in a legal vacuum. They could easily interpret CPA Order No. 17 as a carte blanche. De facto immunity ended when Iraq became sovereign in June 2004, but the culture of impunity continued.

Some PMSCs behaved quite well, of course, but their exemplary conduct served to highlight those who acted badly. One USAID official spoke highly of a company with whom he worked:

> We hired Kroll, from a British base. They were former SAS [Special Air Service] guys. Other than some management problems, overall they did a pretty good—an excellent job . . . They learned how to keep a low profile. Now these other guys: Triple Canopy, Blackwater, etc.? They don't change their tactics . . . Kroll learned how to work with us. They were more controllable. [Their] guys on the ground did well. . . . With Kroll it was not a problem. They kept guns in the car.[47]

It may well be that far more PMSCs behave liked Kroll than like Blackwater. More than a few bad apples, however, easily spoiled the bunch in the eyes of the Iraqi people.

Although the bad behavior of so many security contractors would seem to suggest that PMSCs routinely hired ill-disciplined people prone to going off the reservation, nothing could be further from the truth. Erik Prince, founder and chief executive officer of Blackwater USA, is a former Navy SEAL, who hired many operatives from the Special Forces community. Many other PMSCs also hired former Green Berets, SEALs, and British Special Air Service (SAS) members. Even those employees who had only served in the regular forces had often enjoyed distinguished military careers. Under different circumstances, they probably would have acted more professionally and shown greater restraint. Unfortunately, discipline and professionalism stem only in part from the character and ethos of the individual. The institutional culture in which they operate also shapes behavior, and in Iraq, PMSC corporate culture was overly permissive. Journalist Brian Bennett provided what may be the most balanced assessment of PMSCs. "Conversations with current and former guns for hire paint a picture of a world unique unto itself: insular, tribal, wary of the limelight, competitive and, for the most part, highly professional," he concluded:

> The contractors--and they are almost all men--tend to be former soldiers and come from the U.S., as well as Britain, Ireland, South Africa, Nepal, Fiji, Russia, Australia, Chile and Peru. Their motivations vary from a thirst for adventure to a desire for a nest egg (or to pay down debt) to a refracted form of patriotism.[48]

Considering the mixed motivations of their operatives, the corporate culture of some PMSCs may actually have encouraged abuse. Writing for the *Observer* (UK) in April 2005, journalist Mark Townsend revealed contents of a damning internal communication sent by Blackwater executive Gary Jackson. In the company's March 7 electronic newsletter, Jackson told employees that terrorists "need to get creamed, and it's fun, meaning satisfying, to do the shooting of such folk."[49] With this sort of attitude being expressed by senior company officials, it should come as no surprise that company personnel often failed to distinguish between terrorists and innocent Iraqi civilians.

Lack of oversight and the nature of the environment in which security contractors operated exacerbated this dangerous laxity. A 2008 Human Rights Watch Report described the unhealthy mix of stress and lax supervision that led to so much mischief in Iraq. "Most private security contractors can be expected to do their jobs conscientiously and courageously," the report concluded:

> But they operate in an environment in which the U.S. government has failed to develop the capacity, resources, or legal framework to discipline or punish those contractors who commit serious crimes. The dangers faced by these private security contractors, and the daily stresses caused by those dangers, make it all the more important to keep these forces under control and to have effective means of enforcing discipline.[50]

A narrow focus on the terms of their contract with little consideration of the larger mission in which they performed their duties further encouraged a cavalier attitude toward the local people. U.S. Army Colonel Peter Mansoor complained that PMSC personnel did not realize and/or did not care how the manner in which they completed their specific task might hurt the overall COIN operation. "If they push traffic off the roads or if they shoot up a car that looks suspicious, whatever it may be," he noted, "they may be operating within their contract—to the detriment of the mission, which is to bring the people over to your side."[51] As one contactor put it more bluntly, "Our mission is to protect the principal at all costs. If that means pissing off the Iraqis, too bad."[52]

Employment of local Iraqis by some PMSCs also encouraged heavy handedness. Iraq is a country with deep divisions along ethnic and religious lines. Resentment among the majority Shi'a population and the minority Kurds after years of persecution by Saddam Hussein and the Sunni minority run deep. Using members of one community as security personnel in another meant accepting the risk of guards and escorts abusing people who were not members of their group. In 2005, four American contractors told NBC news of incidents involving abuse of Iraqis by young, poorly trained Kurds hired by Custer Battle Group. The Americans watched as the guards opened fire on innocent civilians and ran one over with a truck.[53]

Contractors also became embroiled in the sordid affair at Abu Ghraib prison. The details of the prisoner abuse scandal, which included torture and sexual assault, became public in 2004. The military personnel involved faced court martial or administrative discipline. Several were convicted and received punishments ranging from dishonorable discharge to prison sentences. Investigations also found that contractors from CACI and Titan were involved in 10 of 44 documented cases of abuse at the prison.[54] The Fay report that documented the Abu Ghraib incidents mentioned contractors but did not indicate what, if any, role they played in directly perpetrating the abuse.[55] The role of contractors in the prisoner abuse scandal received inadequate attention from investigators. As a result, no contractor has been tried for involvement in these incidents.

Even though their behavior did not reflect that of the vast majority of contractors in Iraq, those who caused trouble compromised the mission in a very specific way. COIN depends on winning the support or at least securing the acquiescence of the local population. Often dubbed "winning hearts and minds," gaining support requires first keeping the civilian population safe and secure and then meeting their basic needs while transitioning from military to civilian rule. When the security forces not only fail to protect people but actually contribute to the violence, they are well on their way to losing the campaign. The behavior of a small number of PMSC personnel adversely affected perceptions of military and civilian mission participants, since the Iraqi people viewed them all as part of the same, deeply resented occupation. One study succinctly summarized the nature of the problem:

> In the eyes of the local Iraqi population there are blurred boundaries between a) foreign armies (who are in Iraq to enforce security); b) international private contractors (who are in Iraq working to a more humanitarian mandate to facilitate post-war recovery); and, c) the private security companies who work for both the occupying army and foreign private contractors.[56]

A Rand Corporation study found that Iraqi civilians perceived contractor incidents of misconduct to be far more prevalent than they, in fact, were. When it comes to forging trust, however, perception is reality, especially in a land in which rumor and conspiracy theories abound. An Iraqi family run off the road by contractors, sworn at, or held at gunpoint would rapidly share their experience with their extended kinship network. "To the extent that Iraqis have a negative view of armed contractors, which can be detrimental to larger U.S. goals in Iraq," the report concluded, "such a view is likely derived from a small number of incidents. Hence, the threshold for survey respondents' firsthand knowledge of PSC mistreatment of civilians does not need to be very high for it to be significant."[57] Incidents involving security contractors thus had a negative impact out of proportion to their actual frequency.

The sheer number of contractors and their involvement in all aspects of the Iraq mission may have also contributed to the negative perception of them by the Iraqi population. With at least as many contractors as Soldiers in country at the height of the conflict, how could Iraqis not see them as a major component of the American-led mission? The bad behavior of some PMSCs could thus easily be generalized to all private security guards and perhaps to contractors in general. "By their [PMSC's] pervasive presence among local police, foreign armies and humanitarian and reconstruction organisations [sic] alike," one study concluded:

> the effect of all the international effort, in the eyes of many Iraqis, whether military or humanitarian, is deemed to be aggressive, exploitative and as such creates more grievances for those who are against the 'foreign occupation'.[58]

Even without the significant number of incidents involving PMSC personnel, Iraqis accustomed to Saddam Hussein's secret police had good reason to fear armed men in civilian clothes.[59]

FIXING THE PROBLEM

Use and management of PMSCs in Iraq evolved throughout the course of the war. Neither the Pentagon nor Congress could ignore the growing chorus of criticism about the conduct of private security personnel, especially when so many complaints came from U.S. military personnel. The rising cost of the war also drew attention to waste, fraud, and abuse in the letting and execution of contracts, which added to mounting pressure on Congress to do something about what seemed an out of control contracting process. PMSC incidents stemmed from problems in two broad areas: oversight and management of personnel, and their legal accountability. Washington slowly began to address these problems, especially after the Nisour Square massacre. In 2008, Congress created the Commission on Wartime Contracting in Iraq and Afghanistan:

> pursuant to Fiscal Year 2008 National Defense Authorization Act (NDAA) Section 841, as an independent, bipartisan organization with a 2-year mission to examine wartime contracting for logistics, reconstruction, and security.[60]

The Commission investigated problems of waste, fraud, and abuse in the two conflicts and took steps to correct them.

The Pentagon also took a number of steps to improve contractor management and oversight. In October 2008, the U.S. Army created the Army Contracting Command with two subordinate commands, the Expeditionary Contracting Command and the Mission and Installation Contracting Command. They also deployed more Primary Contracting Officers (PCOs) to the theater. According to FM 3-100.21 "Authority over contractors is exercised through the contracting officer."[61] The PCOs not only oversaw contractor compliance but provided liaison between contractors and the military.[62] Unfortunately, many contracting officers resided in the United States and were thus in no position to oversee directly the behavior of the contractors for whom they were responsible, never mind liaison between them and the military.

In addition to contractor oversight, coordination of PMSC activities with military operations posed major challenges. Contractors frequently worked under "layers of subcontracting" and often lacked communication equipment capable of interfacing with the military, so commanders often did not know who was working within their area of operations.[63] When the four Blackwater contractors were murdered in Fallujah (2004), the local commander did not even know they had been operating in his battle space.[64] Not until 2009 did the military attempt to track the number of contractors in its employ.[65] The Pentagon did, however, take some steps to improve coordination of contractor activities with those of the military in Iraq. In October 2004, the DoD hired Aegis Defence Security, Ltd., a British firm, to set up a Reconstruction Operations Center with five regional branches in Iraq. The purpose of the Center and its subsidiaries was "to provide situational awareness, develop a common operating picture for contractors and the military, and facilitate coordination between the military contractors."[66] The Multi-National Force - Iraq established procedures for convoys approaching checkpoints and made sure PMSC personnel had the correct phone numbers to contact military commanders in the sectors in which they operated.[67]

Although a step in the right direction, creation of the Reconstruction Operations Center did not solve the problem of coordination. USAID refused to participate, and the DoS developed its own coordination mechanism. As a result, DynCorp, Blackwater, and Triple Canopy remained outside the new system. The Center and its subsidiaries also failed to improve horizontal communication as contractors had to use cell phones to call the military headquarters in their area of operation, but could not communicate easily with other contractors or military units farther down the chain of command.[68] The Multi-National Force - Iraq took a further step toward improving coordination with the establishment of six contractor operations cells throughout the country. These cells, which included contractors working for the DoS and USAID as well as those employed by the DoD, coordinated movement between contractors and the military. Once again, cooperation had its limits. Participation in the cells was mandatory only for the DoD contractors.[69] The unwillingness of other agencies and departments to cooperate with the DoD and one another continued to plague the mission.

Having taken steps to improve oversight and coordination/cooperation, the military moved to improve legal accountability of contractors. Holding PMSC personnel legally accountable for wrongdoing proved the most problematic aspect of managing them. Three broad legal frameworks might have been applied to civilian contractors: the laws of the occupied nation; international law; and the laws of the occupying power. None of these worked in Iraq. CPA Order No. 17 gave contractors immunity from Iraqi law. International law (in particular the law of armed conflict) imposes obligations on an occupying power, while the Geneva Conventions and human rights agreements protect prisoners and civilians from abuse. Enforcement, however, has always been difficult for such international agreements. Who apprehends, tries, and punishes wrongdoers? The Hague Tribunal has successfully prosecuted Bosnian war criminals and indicted Charles Taylor of Liberia, but powerful governments, including that of the United States, have refused to recognize its jurisdiction over their citizens. The status of PMSCs under the laws of war is ambiguous. While classified as civilians entitled to noncombatant status, they nonetheless have engaged in armed conflict that could jeopardize their civilian status. On the other hand, as civilians operating out of uniform and outside the military chain of command, they might not be entitled to prisoner of war status if captured.[70]

U.S. criminal law has also proven ineffective in dealing with contractor misconduct. Efforts to prosecute the Blackwater guards for the Nisour Square massacre illustrate the problems of trying contractors in American courts. Under its standing regulations the DoS required that those involved submit written statements describing the incident and their own role in it. Failure to provide such a statement would have been grounds for termination. On December 8, 2007, a grand jury delivered a 35-count indictment against five Blackwater employees, including charges of manslaughter. In 2009 the District Court for the District of Columbia threw out the indictment on grounds that the contractors had been promised immunity when they gave their statements and thus were protected from self-incrimination, and that witness testimony had been tainted by media accounts of the immunized statements.[71] On April 22, 2011, the District of Columbia Appellate Court reversed the District Court decision and ordered a re-review of witness testimony to see if it was tainted.[72] The U.S. Supreme Court declined to hear a further appeal, so the appellate court ruling stands. However, the court decision does not guarantee that anyone will be tried, let alone brought to justice. "Even under the nuanced review ordered by the appellate court," one legal scholar concluded, "it is unclear whether the government will be able to prove that the compelled statements did not taint the prosecution."[73]

A few U.S. laws and the Uniform Code of Military Justice (UCMJ) might be applied to PMSCs, but each has its problems and limitations. The 1996 War Crimes Act applies to Americans even when their actions occur outside the United States. Prosecution under this statute would, however, have faced the same problems encountered in trying Blackwater contractors under ordinary criminal law. To date, no contractor has been prosecuted under the War Crimes Act. Another statute that might be interpreted to cover contractors, the Military Extraterritorial Jurisdiction Act of 2000 (MEJA), applies to acts committed by "certain members of the Armed Forces and by persons employed by or accompanying the Armed Forces outside the United States."[74] The law states that:

> Whoever engages in conduct outside the United States that would constitute an offense punishable by imprisonment for more than 1 year if the conduct had been engaged in within the special maritime and territorial jurisdiction of the United States—
>
> (1) while employed by or accompanying the Armed Forces outside the United States; or
>
> (2) while a member of the Armed Forces subject to chapter 47 of title 10 (the Uniform Code of Military Justice), shall be punished as provided for that offense.[75]

Depending upon how one interprets the nature of the mission, "MEJA does not appear to cover civilian and contract employees of agencies engaged in their own operations overseas."[76] Since PMSC personnel employed by non-DoD entities have caused the most serious problems, their exclusion is a serious weakness in the law.

The UCMJ, which governs the conduct of military personnel on active duty, might have been extended to cover contractors. However, U.S. Army doctrine in place at the beginning of Operation IRAQI FREEDOM explicitly excluded contractors from the UCMJ. "Contractor employees are not subject to military law under the UCMJ when accompanying U.S. forces, except during a declared war," the manual instructed. "Maintaining discipline of contractor employees is the responsibility of the contractor's management structure, not the military chain of command."[77] Problems with contractors in Iraq, however, led the DoD to reconsider this conclusion. In 2006, the Pentagon issued a new directive stating that it was now DoD policy that:

> 4.1. Members of the DoD Components comply with the law of war during all armed conflicts, however such conflicts are characterized, and in all other military operations.
>
> 4.2. The law of war obligations of the United States are observed and enforced by the DoD Components and DoD contractors assigned to or accompanying deployed Armed Forces.
>
> 4.3. An effective program to prevent violations of the law of war is implemented by the DoD Components.
>
> 4.4. All reportable incidents committed by or against U.S. personnel, enemy persons, or any other individual

are reported promptly, investigated thoroughly, and, where appropriate, remedied by corrective action.

4.5. All reportable incidents are reported through command channels for ultimate transmission to appropriate U.S. Agencies, allied governments, or other appropriate authorities.[78]

This guidance removed the ambiguity over whether international standards and agreements applied to conflicts other than declared wars. It also called for a program to prevent violations, mandated a reporting procedure, instituted a corrective process, and implied that further legal action might be taken by authorities to whom the DoD reported abuse. It did not, however, address the problem of legal jurisdiction for non-DoD contractors.

The 2007 Defense Authorization Act amended the UCMJ so that it would cover "in time of declared war or a contingency operation, persons serving with or accompanying an armed force in the field."[79] Extending the jurisdiction of military courts to civilian contractors during contingency operations, where previously it had applied to them only during a declared war, presented new procedural challenges for the armed forces. In a March 2008 memorandum to the service secretaries and combatant command commanders, Secretary of Defense Robert Gates explained:

The unique nature of this extended UCMJ jurisdiction over civilians requires sound management over when, where, and by whom such jurisdiction is exercised. There is a particular need for clarity regarding the legal framework that should govern a command response to any illegal activities by Department of Defense civilian employees and DoD contractor personnel overseas with our Armed Forces.[80]

Legal experts maintain that UCMJ trials of civilians would probably be subject to challenges on constitutional grounds since courts martial "vary from civilian trials and are not restricted by all of the constitutional requirements applicable to Article III courts."[81]

Constitutional issues notwithstanding, these reforms suffered from a far more serious problem: They applied only to contractors employed by the DoD. As already noted, the most serious incidents involved contractors employed by other departments and agencies. Failure of these entities to cooperate with one another stemmed in part from the turf battles endemic to bureaucracies, but it may also have had a more insidious cause. "[The Department of] State was neither willing nor able to substitute for PSCs [Private Security Companies] either military troops or its own government protection personnel," one expert concluded:

> Hence, State chose not to strengthen limits on uses of PSCs. State executed a Memorandum of Agreement with DoD that clarified the role of military commanders over PSCs in their area. The contemporaneous congressional Defense Authorization Act formalized what State and DoD had agreed. Without State's damage control measures, Congress might have gone further and put in place stronger limits on what high-risk functions PSCs should not perform.[82]

That the Nisour Square massacre occurred after the DoD had begun to implement its reforms indicates the limitations of these improvements.

The newly elected Iraqi government did not stand idly by as Washington wrestled with the contractor controversy. In November 2008, Prime Minister Nuri al-Maliki signed a status of forces agreement with U.S. Ambassador Ryan Crocker. The document dealt primarily with withdrawal of U.S. forces from Iraq in 2011, but it also addressed legal jurisdiction over American contractors. The agreement gave Iraq primary jurisdiction over contractors for "crimes committed outside agreed facilities and areas and outside duty status."[83] Other than the Christmas 2006 shooting, however, most escalation-of-force incidents occurred inside "duty status." At the time of the status of forces agreement, the tide of the insurgency had turned, and contractor presence was declining.

In 2010, the Pentagon took a further step to improve the behavior of contractors. U.S. Joint Forces Command published a *Handbook for Contractors in Contingency Operations.*[84] This manual:

> provides the joint force commander (JFC) and staff with an understanding of laws and policy related to the planning, employment, management, and oversight of Armed Private Security Contractors (APSCs) during contingency operations.[85]

Useful though the manual certainly is, it was written near the very end of the Iraq war, and, once again, did not apply to non-DoD contractors.

The Iraq War revealed all the problems inherent in using PMSC personnel in COIN campaigns. They got into escalation of force incidents more readily than did uniformed military personnel. Their boorish behavior alienated the Iraqi civilians whose trust the coalition sought to win. Those civilians made no distinction between PMSC personnel and Soldiers seeing them as part of the same deeply resented occupation. Efforts by the DoD to improve oversight and management of contractors had a salutary effect, although issues of legal jurisdiction were not fully resolved. Failure of the DoS and USAID to engage in reform to the same extent as the DoD limited effectiveness of the Pentagon improvements. Nonetheless, "Incidents in Iraq began an overall downward trend with the beginning of 2Q CY 2007, correlating to the effects of the change in strategy in Iraq."[86] According to this conclusion, the Nisour Square massacre was an outlier. The cause of the reduction in incidents, however, remains unclear. Better management of contractors may have helped, but the decline in the number of PMSC personnel as the COIN campaign wound down and more trained Iraqi security forces became available may have been the real cause of the decline in incidents.

AFGHANISTAN

As the war in Iraq wound down, the conflict in Afghanistan intensified. In December 2008, newly elected President Barak Obama announced a surge of 30,000 additional troops to fight the Taliban. At the same time, the Pentagon shifted from a counterterrorism strategy focused on killing and capturing terrorists to a COIN strategy based on securing territory. The Army shifted from "clear" to "clear and hold" as the guiding principle of the campaign. As in Iraq, the U.S. military and other government bodies relied heavily upon contractors to free up troops for combat operations. Since September 2007, the number of U.S. employed contractors has consistently exceeded U.S. troop levels in the country. Troop levels peaked at 99,800 in March 2011, while the number of contractors reached its highest level of 117,227 a year later.[87] As of September 2009, 26,000 of these contractors worked for PMSCs, 90 percent of them employed directly by the U.S. Government or subcontracted by other U.S.

employed contractors.[88] The composition of this contingent differed markedly in one vital respect from that deployed in Iraq: Local nationals comprised 75 percent of all security contractors in Afghanistan as opposed to 26 percent in Iraq.[89] Security contractors in Afghanistan performed the same tasks they did in Iraq: protecting personnel, providing static security for installations, and escorting convoys. Because of the long supply routes into Afghanistan and the large number of bases and outposts scattered throughout the country, convoys required large, heavily armed escorts and convoying was particularly hazardous duty. A significant number of security contractors thus had to be devoted to this arduous task.

Since the contractor surge in Afghanistan occurred after the high watermark of the war in Iraq, the lessons learned in the one operation should have transferred to the other. To a certain degree they did, but the situation in the two countries differed in significant ways. "The lessons learned in Iraq are being applied to Afghanistan, but require significant adaptation to the Afghan environment," the Commission on Wartime Contracting concluded. "The more fragmented nature of the geography, smaller troop levels, and multiple command relationships (e.g., [U.S. Forces-Afghanistan] USFOR-A, International Security Assistance Force, and the [North Atlantic Treaty Organization] NATO) and each force's particular adaptations affects the learning curve."[90] The surge of troops led to a concomitant increase in number of contractors that the DoD was not initially well prepared to handle. As of 2009, there was no Army Contracting Command (ACC) in Kabul, so the ACC in Iraq oversaw contracts in Afghanistan.[91] A shortage of Contract Officer's Representatives also created problems.[92]

Over-reliance on locally hired security personnel created the most problems in Afghanistan. As in Iraq, U.S. and other foreign nationals engaged in their share of boorish behavior.[93] The most serious incidents, however, involved poorly trained Afghans who often had divided loyalties. PMSCs such as ArmorGroup International did not hire Afghans individually but contracted directly with warlords, who provided the requisite contingent of security guards.[94] The guards, of course, remained loyal to the warlords, who reaped most of the profits from the contract. In some cases, warlords actually supported the Taliban, so American tax dollars helped to fund the very insurgents U.S. forces sought to defeat.[95] In some cases, the warlords not only funneled contract money to the Taliban, but used the security guards they provided to gather intelligence on coalition forces for the insurgents.[96] According to its own internal report, in December 2007, ArmorGroup fired security guards at a base it had been hired to protect because the men had been sharing information "regarding our movements to and from Herat, the routine of the airfield security" with a pro-Taliban warlord and "attempting to coerce fellow members of the guard that they should join with [the warlord]."[97] A raid on another pro-Taliban warlord revealed that some of his men had also been employed by a PMSC.[98] One particularly egregious case illustrates the seriousness of the problem:

In late 2007, the Combined Security Transition Command-Afghanistan (CSTC-A) selected Adraskan to be the site of a new National Training Center (NTC) for the Afghanistan National Civil Order of Police (ANCOP). On January 5, 2008, the U.S. Army awarded EODT [EOD Technology, Inc.] the nearly-$7 million contract to provide site security at the Adraskan NTC. To staff its guard force, EODT assigned quotas to local strongmen or 'notables.' What was most 'notable' about the men, however, was their reported affiliation with criminal and anti-Coalition activities.[99]

PMSCs providing convoy escorts engaged in equally blatant abuses of their contracts. They ostensibly paid warlords to provide security for convoys passing through the warlord's territory. A June 2010 congressional report, appropriately titled *Warlord Inc.: Extortion and Corruption along the U.S. Supply Chain in Afghanistan*, presented a scathing exposé of the problem.[100] Most supplies come by road from the port of Karachi, Pakistan, almost 868 miles from Kabul, over poor roads through difficult terrain in a hostile environment. Keeping this route open, while maintaining a distribution network to bases throughout the country, presented an enormous logistical challenge. To meet this challenge, the DoD employed a new approach known as host nation contracting by which responsibility for transporting supplies along a route is "almost entirely outsourced to local truckers and Afghan private security providers."[101] This approach has created widespread opportunities for abuse as oversight of contractors and their employees has been very difficult. The congressional report accused warlords through whose territory convoys had to pass of running a giant "protection racket," host nation contractors interviewed referred to these payments as "extortion," "bribes," "special security," and/or "protection payments."[102] The report identified such payments as "a significant potential source of funding for the Taliban."[103]

The practice of paying protection money has had other deleterious side effects. COIN requires building state institutions and strengthening government sovereignty over insurgents who seek to undermine both.

Putting more money into the hands of local warlords has had the opposite effect. It has exacerbated the problem of shadow or alternative governance, a phenomenon by which nonstate entities exercise control over areas of territory within a sovereign state and impose their own system of governance over it.[104] The Taliban, for example, have established alternative courts that have earned a reputation for greater fairness in resolving ordinary civil disputes than the official Afghan courts notorious for their corruption.[105] Paying warlords to "protect" convoys passing through their area has actually enhanced the deleterious effects of shadow governance, strengthening their power base at the expense of the national government.[106]

In addition to strengthening warlords, the contractors themselves have become a power center, further eroding national sovereignty. A May 2010 background paper published by the Institute for the Study of War drew attention to this problem in southern Afghanistan. "Because PSCs are under the control of powerful individuals, rather than the Afghan National Security Forces," the paper concluded, "they compete with state security forces and interfere with a government monopoly on the use of force."[107] PMSCs may further undermine security by syphoning talent from the Afghan National Police and Army. Police chiefs commonly have their men work for security contractors to supplement their income.[108] Escorting convoys or guarding facilities takes these officers away from their primary police duties.

In his second inaugural address, Afghan President Hamid Karzai specifically addressed the problems caused by security contractors. "The goal of a powerful national government can be realized by the stronger presence of national security forces in all parts of the country," he declared. "Within the next 2 years, we want operations by all private national and international security firms to be ended and their duties delegated to Afghan security entities."[109] Implementing this recommendation, however, will prove exceedingly difficult as it will require taking on powerful local contractors, including members of the president's own family.[110]

In addition to the problems of corruption and shadow governance fueled by U.S. contracts, escalation-of-force incidents involving security contractors occurred in Afghanistan just as they had in Iraq. So did friendly fire incidents, in which contractors shot at American Soldiers. The preponderance of poorly trained locally hired PMSC personnel exacerbated these problems. Once again, convoy escorts proved particularly problematic. An Associated Press story from April 2010 was scathingly critical of trigger-happy security guards in Kandahar province. "Private Afghan security guards protecting NATO supply convoys in southern Kandahar province regularly fire wildly into villages they pass," the article noted, "hindering coalition efforts to build local support ahead of this summer's planned offensive in the area, U.S. and Afghan officials say."[111] A U.S. Army captain quoted in the story corroborated this conclusion: "Especially as they go through the populated areas, they tend to squeeze the trigger first and ask questions later."[112] Besides being poorly trained, the convoy escorts were also often high on heroin or hashish.[113] As was the case in Iraq, Afghanis make no distinction between PMSC personnel and American Soldiers. They see them both as part of the same unwanted occupation.

Poor training further hampered the performance of local security contractors in Afghanistan. Lack of adequate oversight and annual performance reviews allowed this problem to persist. A congressional over-sight committee drew attention to the matter in one of its reports:

> Between 2007 and 2009, DOD had in excess of 125 di-rect contracts with more than 70 entities to perform security in Afghanistan. Frequently, those contracts were to provide security at U.S. forward operating bases (FOBs). The Committee found that many con-tract files lacked information on contractors' capabili-ties or past performance and contained no information about how contractors performed on the job. Where performance was examined, DOD documents fre-quently revealed significant gaps between contractor performance and DOD and CENTCOM [U.S. Central Command] standards.[114]

The report also noted that a March 2009 audit of one contractor found "no evidence of annual qualification of safe handling of firearms" and "no annual training records for Rules of Use of Force (RUF) and Laws of Armed Conflict," even though DoD rules required this training.[115]

While local contractors created the most problems, foreign employees (U.S., British, etc.) also got into trouble. Speaking on condition of anonymity, one US-AID official described the same intimidating tactics and boorish behavior that were evident in Iraq:

> DynCorp, Kroll, Global, and their operations are in Afghanistan. The way that they behave in public is quite offensive by any standard. In a small town, they drive quickly; shooters shoot at traffic; they force their cars through. That is not only when they are escorting the Ambassador. It is also when they are just driving around town or to the airport. I questioned them on a number of occasions. They think that it is harder for a suicide bomber to kill you if you are driving very

quickly and weaving through traffic. So they think of it as a safety precaution. It's not clear to me that this is true. This is an excellent example of misplacing our priorities. . . . They exhibit a level of arrogance that is just difficult to describe unless you actually view it. . . . Fear is contrary to our interest. In the last 4 years, people have been forced to flee for their lives in the face of U.S. security vehicles. It is not the military that drives like that . . . there have been hundreds of times that I've seen PMCs do it. They behave in public in a threatening manner. It is part of their rules of engagement. Many of the shooters were decent guys. At the same time, as of July 2005, these kinds of intimidating incidents happened all the time.[116]

U.S. Government departments and agencies in Afghanistan thus experienced many of the same problems with contractors as they encountered in Iraq as well as some new ones. Over-reliance on locally hired security personnel caused far more problems than it had in Iraq, largely because the local hires represented a much larger percentage of the contractor force. The difficult terrain; the complex web of family, clan, and tribal loyalties; poor infrastructure; and weak central government have increased the challenges of the International Security Assistance Force (ISAF) mission and made effective use of contractors more difficult.

LESSONS FROM IRAQ AND AFGHANISTAN

Every war or contingency operation is unique. The wars in Afghanistan and Iraq occurred in different geographic, social, economic, and political environments that shaped how they were fought. These differences also affected how the U.S. Government employed contractors and the problems it encountered in using them effectively. These differences notwithstanding, the two campaigns yield some consistent lessons on the use of PMSCs in contingency operations. Properly analyzed, these lessons form the basis of recommendations to improve the use of contractors in future operations.

Lesson 1: Escorts Cause the Biggest Problems.

In both Iraq and Afghanistan, security contractors escorting supply convoys or motorcades carrying personnel they were tasked to protect have been the most prone to getting into escalation of force incidents. In Iraq, the biggest offenders were the personal security details of CPA and other U.S. Government employees. In Afghanistan, supply convoy escorts have caused the most problems. Moving goods or people through difficult terrain occupied by local inhabitants who resent the presence of foreign troops in their country is incredibly difficult. PMSC personnel, focused narrowly on the terms of their contract with little understanding of, or regard for, larger mission objectives, have tended to fire at anyone whom they saw as a potential threat to the goods or people they were escorting. This tendency to shoot first and ask questions later increases during a COIN campaign in which identifying insurgents amid a sullen civilian population proves difficult. Even highly trained professional Soldiers find it hard to exercise restraint in such a combat environment. Highly paid contractors with de facto legal immunity are not highly motivated even to try to make such a distinction. Poorly trained, locally hired guards hardly bother at all, especially if those they are shooting at belong to a different ethnic or social group.

Lesson 2: Local People Make No Distinction between American Soldiers and Armed Civilian Contractors.

By all accounts, military personnel in Iraq and Afghanistan have behaved far better than PMSC personnel. Despite some serious incidents, American Soldiers and Marines have generally exercised commendable restraint because of the institutional culture in which they operate, the legal accountability they face under the UCMJ, and their understanding of COIN. They have been among the most vocal critics of PMSC behavior. Unfortunately, local people do not distinguish between American Soldiers and contractors. Both belong to the same mission, so bad behavior by one tarnishes the reputation of the other.

Lesson 3: Training and Experience Matter but Are Not Sufficient to Ensure Good Behavior.

Inexperienced, poorly trained PMSC personnel did cause serious problems in both Iraq and Afghanistan. Training and experience should, therefore, be required of all PMSCs employed directly by U.S. Government departments and agencies as well as security personnel employed as subcontractors by U.S. Government contractors. Training and experience alone, however, provide no guarantee of good behavior. Blackwater USA employed some of the most experienced and highly trained security guards, including former Special Forces members. Despite the expertise of its employees, the company also became embroiled in some of the most notorious escalation-of-force incidents in Iraq. Institutional culture shapes human behavior at least as much, and perhaps more, than does personal ethics and professionalism. Blackwater and other companies allowed or perhaps even encouraged an overly permissive attitude toward the use of force. This permissiveness had disastrous consequences.

Lesson 4: Local Security Personnel often Lack Neutrality.

Contingency operations often occur in countries with deep ethnic and/or religious divisions. Hiring local security guards from one group thus frequently creates problems, as these guards may mistreat members from another group. Afghanis hired to protect installations or escort convoys usually owed primary allegiance to some warlord or local leader. In some cases, these warlords even supported the Taliban. Although less common in Iraq, instances of guards from one ethnic group abusing civilians from another did occur. Kurdish guards have been accused of heavy-handedness by Sunni and Shi'a Iraqis.

Lesson 5: Hiring Local Security Personnel May Undermine Sovereignty.

COIN requires strengthening a threatened state so that it can govern more effectively, win the trust (or at least the acceptance) of its own people, and defeat the insurgents. In Afghanistan, hiring local tribesmen to escort convoys and guard compounds has strengthened local warlords, perhaps taking away potential recruits from the security forces and undermining the sovereignty of the Afghan government. It has also funneled money to the Taliban. The process of contracting directly with warlords for contingents of security guards has thus undermined the COIN campaign.

Lesson 6: Current Law Is Inadequate for Holding Contractors Accountable.

Local, international, and U.S. law have proven inadequate for holding contractors accountable for their actions in contingency operations. The limited number of prosecutions and the virtual absence of convictions for violations committed in both Iraq and Afghanistan despite numerous incidents of wrongdoing clearly indicate that no existing legal system works well for regulating PMSCs operating in the grey area of contingency operations. The UCMJ may be applicable to DoD contractors, but it cannot be applied to contractors working for the DoS, USAID, and other civilian departments and agencies. The United States understandably has been reluctant to allow its citizens to be tried in host nation courts for fear of malicious prosecutions and lack of safeguards to protect the rights of the accused. International law has been equally problematic as has U.S. criminal law in general and specific acts such as the MEJA in particular.

Lesson 7: PMSCs Do Not Adversely Affect Army Retention Rates.

Many analysts and military officers worried that deployment of large numbers of PMSC personnel to Iraq and Afghanistan would adversely affect re-enlistment of American Soldiers. The higher pay of civilian security contractors would, they feared, syphon off talent from the regular forces in general and the Special Forces in particular. "Why re-enlist," the argument went, "when you can make at least twice as much working for a PMSC?" Fortunately for the U.S. military, this has not proven to be the case. A study

conducted by Ryan Kelly found that American Soldiers working alongside contractors perceived that
the higher pay the contractors received, along with
the more relaxed atmosphere in which they worked,
would adversely affect retention and unit cohesion.
His study also found, however, that despite these perceptions, the presence of highly paid contractors in
their area of operations did not, in reality, adversely
affect Soldiers' commitment to remaining in the service. Whether unit cohesion was adversely affected
was less clear.[117]

Military continuation rates have remained fairly
consistent throughout the Iraq War.[118] Large re-enlistment bonuses, however, probably contributed to
retention, especially for younger service personnel:

> Such bonuses may counteract the negative effects of
> PSC employment on military retention. Therefore,
> while these new retention figures for early-career sol-
> diers may foreshadow a growing trend for troops to
> opt for continued military service rather than depar-
> ture to a private security firm, recent research on these
> topics also indicates that maintaining fairly steady
> retention and continuation rates in the modern era
> of frequent military deployments will likely come at
> greater cost to the taxpayer.[119]

**Lesson 8: The Contracting Process Increases the
U.S. Footprint, Creating a Need for More PMSCs.**

No-bid, cost-plus contracting creates a bigger-is-
better mentality. Contractors who build bases and run
their support facilities have a powerful incentive to increase the size and complexity of the goods and services they provide. The more extensive the facilities they
build and staff, the greater the quantity and variety of

food they serve, the more money they make. Unfortunately, by increasing the size of the U.S. footprint in a contingency operation, contractors also increase the need for PMSC personnel. Larger bases require more guards, and more elaborate menus mean more supply convoys and, therefore, more armed escorts to protect them.[120] More escorts create more opportunities for incidents to occur. The Blackwater contractors killed in Fallujah in 2004 were delivering kitchen utensils.

Lesson 9: Lack of Coordination and Cooperation Plague Employment of PMSCs.

Successful COIN requires unity of effort, which, in turn, entails close cooperation among all those engaged in the campaign. The plethora of U.S. and allied government departments and agencies, NGOs, IOs, and private individuals hiring security contractors added to the complexity of operations in both Iraq and Afghanistan. In Afghanistan, the presence of a coalition with many more participants, ISAF, has exacerbated the problem. While the DoD has taken steps to improve coordination among contractors and between them and the military, it has had limited success eliciting cooperation from the DoS, USAID, and other entities, never mind those not working for the U.S. Government. Unity of effort has bedeviled contingency operations since the Bosnian mission, and the introduction of PMSCs to the mix adds but one more element to an already complicated order of battle.

RECOMMENDATIONS

Identifying mistakes made in past missions is much easier than making recommendations to prevent them recurring in future ones. Reviewing the long list of escalation-of-force incidents involving armed contractors in Iraq and Afghanistan and considering the numerous other problems all types of contractors have caused, it would be tempting to conclude that the U.S. Government should eschew use of contractors in combat zones. Such an approach would not be feasible, however, even if it were desirable. Contractors have become a vital part of the total-force structure. No one wants to go back to the days when Soldiers peeled potatoes between combat operations. As previously noted, logistics and support contractors cause relatively few problems, although they need better oversight and management to prevent waste, fraud, and abuse; and they should not be allowed to increase the size of the mission footprint unnecessarily. Use of PMSCs in contingency operations, especially COIN campaigns, however, needs to be reconsidered. The following recommendations derived from the lessons discussed in this monograph identify steps that might be taken to make employment of contractors in contingency operations more effective.

Recommendation 1: Assign PMSC Roles Based Upon Risk Analysis.

The standard for determining what armed civilian contractors may and may not do has been based upon the "inherently governmental" principle. Those tasks designated as inherently governmental may not be performed by private sector employees. Direct involvement in combat operations is clearly an inherently governmental function, which civilian contractors may not do, while serving food in a mess hall obviously is not. Such clear distinctions work well enough in peace time and during conventional wars, but they have proven highly problematic during contingency operations in which the boundary between combat and noncombat activities becomes blurred. There are no rear areas in an insurgency. Everyone outside the wire of fortified bases may at any moment find themselves in a combat situation. Insurgents, in fact, prefer to attack the weaker "tail" of an expeditionary force rather than its sharp "teeth."

Because of the ambiguous nature of roles and missions in COIN campaigns and other contingency operations, the government should adopt a risk-based assessment of roles and missions. This approach would designate as "inherently governmental" tasks with a high risk of bringing those who perform them into violent contact with insurgents or civilian noncombatants.[121] It would allow the DoD, DoS, USAID, and other entities to take into account the unique situation of each operational environment. Driving a truck would be a high-risk activity in Afghanistan, but not in Kosovo. Providing static perimeter security for a construction site would be high-risk in Iraq, but not in Bosnia. For consistency, this approach to task assessment would have to apply to all contractors and subcontractors within an area of operation.

Linking task designation to risk would have significant manpower implications for the armed forces. The Army, for example, might need to resume responsibility for convoy escorts in some conflict areas and/or during some phases of an operation. If doing so reduced escalation of force incidents which fuel insurgency, however, there might be a long-term saving for a short-term expense. Fewer incidents of civilians being killed by out-of-control contractors might help U.S. forces and the threatened government to resolve the insurgency sooner rather than later. Other agencies would have to follow the same guidelines as the DoD. The Bureau of Diplomatic Security (BDS), which protects DoS personnel, would thus need to increase its capability. The shortage of BDS personnel forced the DoS to hire Blackwater for personnel protection details. Rather than bear the cost of a permanently enhanced security bureau, the BDS could acquire a surge capacity by developing a mechanism for hiring short-term contract security personnel directly instead of turning to PMSCs in a crisis. USAID would need to develop a similar approach to personnel protection.

Subcontractors, NGOs, and IOs present a unique challenge. Providing military escorts to companies such as Halliburton, which hires security guards to escort convoys and protect construction sites, would be labor intensive and expensive. Requiring that PMSC subcontractors be subject to U.S. military oversight and jurisdiction would, however, address the problem of oversight and accountability. Although it would be politically controversial, the U.S. military could impose the same requirement on NGOs, IOs, and anyone else working in the American area of operations. Anyone carrying a gun in the area of operations should be answerable to the force commander.

Recommendation 2: Improve Legal Accountability of Armed Contractors.

Efforts to extend the jurisdiction of existing laws such as the UCMJ and Military Extraterritorial Judicial Act have met with limited success or have yet to be tested. Conviction of a civilian contractor under the UCMJ might not, for example, withstand an appeal based on constitutional grounds.[122] The best solution would be to pass a law applying specifically to contractors accompanying U.S. forces during contingency operations. In the opinion of one legal expert:

> The paramount legal question is how to regulate private corporate entities, which provide state-based military functions. The clear answer is that there must be some framework which recognizes the unique attributes of the PCMF [Privately Contracted Military Firm, another term for PMSC] and accordingly attaches status and legal accountability thereto.[123]

Once these laws were passed, contractors could be required to adhere to them through signing consent agreements as part of the contracting process.

Another solution to the problem of legal accountability would be to make use of "forum selection clauses." Such clauses are frequently used in cases where a contractor may be subject to conflicting legal jurisdictions. Blackwater personnel might have faced criminal and civil prosecution in both Iraqi and U.S. courts, but they have not been held accountable in either. A forum selection clause would specify in the contract under which jurisdiction the contractor came. Such a clause "would be universally recognized by judicial tribunals, whether national or international," one legal expert concludes:

> The enforceability of such pre-dispute agreements for civil claims is by now well-established in U.S. domestic law and international law, except where there is evident fraud or gross disparity in bargaining power between the parties.[124]

Forum selection clauses have the advantage of making use of existing laws rather than relying on passage of new legislation.

Recommendation 3: Improve Interagency Cooperation.

Lack of cooperation between government agencies is the *bête noir* of joint operations. Turf battles and bureaucratic stove-piping often prevent unity of effort among U.S. departments and agencies. Coalition partners, NGOs, and IOs increase these problems exponentially. PMSCs add yet another layer of complexity to contingency operations. The DoD has taken useful steps to improve coordination in Iraq, and the DoS cooperated in the process to some extent. There was, however, no way to compel disparate contractors to work together. The CPA might have been in a position to coerce compliance, since it was the de facto government of occupied Iraq, but neither ISAF nor the DoD could do so in Afghanistan, which has had an elected government throughout most of the war. Only congressional oversight and strong leadership from the executive branch can force interagency cooperation and even then, as the example of the Department of Homeland Security demonstrates, subsidiary agencies and departments will still guard their turf tenaciously.

Recommendation 4: Improve Contractor Oversight.

The U.S. Army has made great strides in improving oversight of contractors in the field. It has created an Army Contracting Command and increased the number of Primary Contracting Officers (PCOs). It also deploys PCOs to the area of operations to improve oversight and facilitate cooperation between PMSCs and the military. USAID, the DoS, and other government entities must take similar steps. Audits to ensure compliance with the terms of the contract and U.S. Government regulations such as weapons qualification must be performed on a regular basis. Subcontracting of PMSCs by primary contractors should be subject to direct oversight by PCOs. Anyone carrying a gun in a U.S. military area of operation should thus be answerable to the force commander.

Recommendation 5: Avoid Employing Locals as Security Guards.

Local employees have been a source of difficulty in Iraq and a major problem in Afghanistan. Using them as security guards has some advantages but also many disadvantages. On the one hand, they know the area and its people and speak the local language; on the other, they are often poorly trained and enmeshed in the social system in which the conflict that the U.S. intervention is trying to end takes place. Guards from one ethnic or religious group often abuse members of other groups.

Hiring locals can be a useful COIN strategy. It infuses money into the local economy, improves quality of life, and builds trust. If the locally hired employees weaken state sovereignty and/or use excessive force, they undermine the COIN campaign. For this reason, U.S. contractors and subcontractors should be prohibited from hiring locals for any but the most restricted security roles. Pashtuns, with the help of U.S. Special Forces Teams, have been effective in defending their own villages, but they have not done well as convoy escorts or guards at facilities. The practice of contracting with a warlord or any other local leader should be abolished. PMSCs must vet and hire their own personnel directly and on an individual basis.

Recommendation 6: Do Not Allow Contractors to Enlarge the Mission Footprint.

No-bid, cost plus contracts, and the desire to avoid deploying more troops allowed contracting in Iraq to get out of hand. Although logistics and support contractors seldom came into direct conflict with insurgents or harmed innocent civilians, they contributed indirectly to the proliferation of security contractors. The contracting system encouraged a more-is-better approach to base construction and supply. Large bases required more guards. More supplies meant more convoys, and more convoys required more security escorts. More escorts meant more opportunities for escalation-of-force incidents. Contingency operations work best when the U.S. footprint is as small as possible.[125] An occupation force is always resented, so it makes sense to keep its numbers as small possible. In addition to requiring more security, large bases with all the conveniences of home isolate U.S. Soldiers from the people they are trying to help. As P.W. Singer so aptly observed:

> Turning logistics and operations into a for-profit endeavor helped feed the 'Green Zone' mentality problem of sprawling bases, which runs counter to everything General Petraeus pointed to as necessary to winning a counterinsurgency in the new Army/ USMC manual he helped write.[126]

Recommendation 7: Stop Use of Contractors for "Workarounds."

The final recommendation has less to do with the conduct of campaigns than it does with the more important issue of government accountability. A strong case can be made that PMSCs have been used to enhance executive power and avoid accountability. The term "workaround" refers to a process by which executives acquire:

> the means of accomplishing distinct policy goals that—but for the pretext of technocratic privatization—would either be legally unattainable or much more difficult to realize. In short, they are executive aggrandizing. They enable Presidents, governors, and mayors to exercise greater unilateral policy discretion—at the expense of legislators, courts, successor administrations, and the people.[127]

This "aggrandizing" can be hard to spot in the midst of a mission in which outsourcing certain roles and tasks looks like a mere cost-saving measure that allows government to hire the personnel to meet a short-term need rather than permanently increase military manpower for an occasional contingency. What happened in Iraq illustrates the problem:

> For a military engagement of waning popularity, the Pentagon needs 400,000 troops; realistically, it has less than half that number available. But, the Pentagon is able to work around the shortfall by calling forth a phalanx of private contractors. As a result of the private recruitment, these contractors, who are far less visible to the American public, serve at a roughly 1-to-1 ratio with US military personnel. Their presence dilutes body counts (as contractor fatalities are

not officially tallied or publicly announced) and thus obscures the full extent of the human costs of war. Their presence also allows the government to avoid politically difficult policy decisions regarding whether to withdraw, scale back the engagement, reinstitute a civilian draft, or seek outside support from a broader coalition of willing international partners.[128]

To stop this potential abuse of executive power, Congress must increase its oversight of the contracting process. Current oversight focuses on problems of waste, fraud, and abuse rather than on the policy implications of using contractors in place of military personnel.

CONCLUSION: IMPLICATIONS FOR U.S. LAND FORCES

While doing away with logistics and support contractors would have profound implications for U.S. Landpower, reducing or eliminating PMSCs would not. The Army could not function at its current level of readiness without logistics and support contractors. This contracting can save money on a regular basis and provide a surge capacity in the event of a contingency operation. Resuming direct responsibility for transport, dining facilities, and a host of other functions would cost more than the Pentagon could afford. The DoD would have to increase troop levels or compromise combat readiness. In absence of a dire emergency, the U.S. taxpayers will not welcome increases in military spending for more troops. Assigning Soldiers to support roles now performed by contractors would decrease the Army's ability to perform its core tasks. Increasing reliance on hi-tech weapons systems that require extensive training to operate means that giving up Soldiers to KP duty is more problematic than it was when low-tech infantry made up the bulk of U.S. ground forces. Contractors also provide essential maintenance support for sophisticated weapons systems.

As much as it needs logistics and support contractors, however, the Army does not depend nearly so much upon PMSCs. Soldiers can guard their own bases and provide their own personnel protection details. Only in the case of supply convoys and protection of forward operating bases in Afghanistan have they relied heavily on private security personnel. That reliance has had such negative consequences that it should be reconsidered. Although performing these functions would require the military to deploy more of its manpower, this short-term cost might result in long-term saving. Contracting out a function to free up Soldiers for combat duty makes no sense if the contractors make the insurgency worse and thus increase the need for more Soldiers. The Army could still employ civilian drivers, perhaps even local ones, but it should not outsource armed escort duties or other high risk activities. The whole point of outsourcing is not merely to save money, but to increase the likelihood that an operation will succeed in a timely manner.

ENDNOTES

1. See account of the Fallujah ambush in Jeremy Scahill, *Blackwater: The Rise of the World's Most Powerful Mercenary Army*, New York: Nation Books, 1st ed., 2007, pp. 164-167.

2. *Ibid.*, p. 10.

3. *Ibid.*, pp. 3-9.

4. David Johnston and John M. Broder, "F.B.I. Says Guards Killed 14 Iraqis Without Cause," *New York Times* online, November 14, 2007, available from *www.nytimes.com/2007/11/14/world/ middleeast/14blackwater.html?pagewanted=1&_r=0.*

5. The subtitle of Scahill's book, *The Rise of the World's Most Powerful Mercenary Army*, illustrates the tendency to hyperbole even in serious works as does the title of Robert Young Pelton's work, *Licensed to Kill: Hired Guns in the War on Terror*, New York: Three Rivers Press, 2006.

6. Federal Inventories Reform Act of 1998, Public Law 105-270, Section 5.2.A.

7. Don Mayer, "Peaceful Warriors: Private Military Security Companies and the Quest for Stable Societies," *Journal of Business Ethics*, Vol. 89, Spring 2010, p. 389.

8. Sid Ellington, "The Rise of Battlefield Private Contractors," *Public Integrity*, Vol. 13, No. 2, Spring 2011, p. 136.

9. P. W. Singer, *Corporate Warriors: The Rise of the Military Industry*, London, UK: Cornell, 2003, pp. 66-67.

10. Ellington, pp. 138-139.

11. *Protocol Additional to the Geneva Conventions of 12 August 1949, and Relating to the Protection of Victims of International Armed Conflicts, Protocol I*, June 1977, p. 8, available from *www.icrc.org/ applic/ihl/ihl.nsf/Article.xsp?action=openDocument&documentId=9E DC5096D2C036E9C12563CD0051DC30.*

12. "International Convention Against the Recruitment, Use, Financing and Training of Mercenaries," UN Resolution A/ RES/44/34, December 14, 1989.

13. For detailed discussion of pre-invasion planning, see Michael R. Gordon and Bernard E. Trainor, *Cobra II: The Inside Story of the Invasion and Occupation of Iraq*, New York: Vintage Books, 2007.

14. For discussion of this planning and mindset, see Thomas R. Mockaitis, *Iraq and the Challenge of Counterinsurgency*, Westport, CT: Praeger, 2008.

15. Singer, *Corporate Warriors*, pp. 244-245.

16. Deborah D. Avant and Renée de Nevers, "Military Contractors & the American Way of War," *Dædalus, the Journal of the American Academy of Arts & Sciences*, Vol. 140, No. 3, Summer 2011, p. 94.

17. Singer, *Corporate Warriors*, p. 245.

18. Avant and Nevers, p. 94.

19. *Ibid.*

20. David Perry, "Blackwater vs. Bin Laden: the Private Sector's Role in American Counterterrorism," *Comparative Strategy*, Vol. 31, Issue 1, 2012, p. 44.

21. *Contractors Support of U.S. Operations in Iraq*, Washington, DC: Congressional Budget Office, 2008, p. 1.

22. Sarah Cotton *et al.*, *Hired Guns: Views about Armed Contractors in Operation Iraqi Freedom*, Santa Monica, CA: Rand, 2010, p. 12.

23. Singer, *Corporate Warriors*, p. 245.

24. Cotton *et al.*, p. 14.

25. *Contractors Support of U.S. Operations in Iraq*, p. 9.

26. *Ibid.*, p. 8.

27. *Ibid.*, p. 9.

28. *Ibid.*

29. *Contractors on the Battlefield*, Arlington, VA: Lexington Institute, 2007, p. 4.

30. Jonathan Starry, "What Did Contractors Do in Iraq?" Overview Project, February 21, 2012, available from *overview. ap.org/blog/2012/02/iraq-security-contractors/*.

31. *Ibid.*

32. *Ibid.*

33. Quoted in *Ibid.*

34. *Ibid.*

35. Cotton *et al.*, p. xv.

36. Memorandum on Additional Information about Blackwater USA, from Majority Staff to U.S. House of Representatives Committee on Oversight and Reform, October 1, 2007, available from *www.npr.org/documents/2007/oct/house_blackwater.pdf*.

37. Steve Fainaru, "Guards in Iraq Cite Frequent Shootings. Companies Seldom Report Incidents, U.S. Officials Say," *Washington Post*, October 3, 2007, online edition, *www.washingtonpost. com/wp-dyn/content/article/2007/10/02/AR2007100202456_pf.html*.

38. Memorandum on Additional Information about Blackwater USA.

39. *Ibid.*

40. Quoted in *Ibid.*

41. Quoted in Scott Horton and Michael McClintock, *Private Security Contractors at War: Ending the Culture of Impunity*, Washington, DC: Human Rights Watch First, 2008, p. 1.

42. *Ibid.*

43. Quoted in Brian Bennett, "America's Other War," *Time*, Vol. 170, Issue 17, October 29, 2007, pp. 30-33.

44. Horton and McClintock, from the title of their report.

45. "Coalition Provisional Order Number 17: Status of Coalition, Foreign Liaison Missions, Their Personnel and Contractors," June 26, 2003.

46. *Field Manual (FM) 3-100.21, Contractors on the Battle Field*, Washington, DC: Headquarters, Department of the Army, 2003, pp. 1-2.

47. Cotton *et al.*, p. 28.

48. Quoted in Bennett, pp. 30-33.

49. Mark Townsend, "Fury at 'shoot for fun' memo," *Observer*, London, UK, April 3, 2005, available from *www.uruknet. info/?p=10865*.

50. Horton and McClintock, p. 6.

51. Quoted in Nathan Hodge, "Revised US Law Spotlights Role of Contractors on Battlefield," *Jane's Defence Weekly*, January 10, 2007, available from *n.privateforces.com/index.php/Legal-Aspects-Regulation/revised-us-law-spotlights-role-of-contractors-on-battlefield.html*.

52. Quoted in Horton and McClintock, p. 71.

53. "U.S. contractors in Iraq allege abuses," NBC News, February 17, 2005, available from *www.nbcnews.com/id/6947745/#. UcusS5wVRHA*.

54. Horton and McClintock, p. 52; incidents are detailed in Major George R. Fay, "AR 15-6 Investigation of the Abu Ghraib Detention Facility and 205th Military Intelligence Brigade, 34-176," August 2004, available from *news.findlaw.com/hdocs/docs/dod/ fay82504rpt.pdf*.

55. *Ibid.*

56. Kjell Bjork and Richard Jones, "Overcoming Dilemmas Created by the 21st Century Mercenaries: Conceptualising the use of Private Security Companies in Iraq," *Third World Quarterly*, Vol. 26, No. 4-5, 2005, pp. 778-779.

57. Cotton *et al.*, p. xv.

58. Bjork and Jones, p. 282.

59. *Ibid.*, p. 787.

60. *Analysis of the Interim Report of the Commission on Wartime Contracting in Iraq and Afghanistan,* Washington, DC: Department of Defense, 2009, p. 1.

61. FM 3-100.21, pp. 1-2.

62. *Ibid.,* pp. 10-11.

63. David Perry, "Blackwater vs. Bin Laden: the Private Sector's Role in American Counterterrorism," *Comparative Strategy,* Vol. 31, Issue 1, 2012, p. 43.

64. *Ibid.*

65. *Ibid.*

66. Ulrich Petershon, "The Other Side of the COIN: Private Security Companies and Counterinsurgency Operations," *Studies in Conflict & Terrorism,* Vol. 34, 2011, p. 786.

67. *Ibid.*

68. *Ibid.*

69. Details on Contractor Operations Cells from *Ibid.,* pp. 786-787.

70. Jennifer K. Elsea, Moshe Schwartz, and Kennon H. Nakamura, *Private Security Contractors in Iraq: Background, Legal Status, and Other Issues,* Washington, DC: Congressional Research Service (CRS), 2008, p. 16.

71. Emily Kelly, "Holding Blackwater Accountable: Private Security Contractors and the Protections of Use Immunity," *Boston College International and Comparative Law Review,* Vol. 35, Issue 3, Electronic Supplement, pp. 20-21.

72. *Ibid.*, p. 21.

73. *Ibid.*, p. 29.

74. "Military Extraterritorial Jurisdiction Act," Public Law 106-53, November 22, 2000, Section 3261.

75. *Ibid.*, Section 3261 a.

76. Elsea *et al.*, p. 24.

77. FM 3-100.21, pp. 4-12.

78. "Department of Defense Directive Number 2311.01E," May 9, 2006, p. 1.

79. Defense Authorization Act, USC § 802 - Art. 2., Persons subject to this chapter, a. 10, October 17, 2006.

80. "Memorandum for Secretaries of Departments, Chairman of Joint Chiefs of Staff, Under Secretaries of Defense, Commanders of Combatant Commands," March 10, 2008.

81. Elsea *et al.*, p. 27.

82. Charles Tiefer, "Restrain 'Risky Business': Treat High-Risk Private Security Contractors as Inherently Governmental," *Harvard Journal on Legislation*, Vol. 50, 2013, p. 217.

83. "Agreement between the Republic of Iraq and the United States of America on the withdrawal of United States Forces from Iraq and the Organization of their Activities during their Temporary Presence in Iraq," November 17, 2008, Article 12, para. 1.

84. *Handbook for Armed Private Security Contractors in Contingency Operations*, Washington, DC: U.S. Joint Forces Command, 2010.

85. *Ibid.*, p. v.

86. *Analysis of the Interim Report of the Commission on Wartime Contracting in Iraq and Afghanistan,* Washington, DC: Department of Defense, 2009, p. 26.

87. Moshe Schwartz and Jennifer Church, *Department of Defense's Use of Contractors to Support Military Operations: Background,* Washington, DC: CRS, 2013, p. 24.

88. *Inquiry into the Role and Oversight of Private Security Contractors in Afghanistan,* Report together with Additional Views of the Committee on Armed Services, U.S. Senate, September 28, 2010, p. i.

89. Schwartz and Church, p. 24.

90. *Analysis of the Interim Report of the Commission on Wartime Contracting in Iraq and Afghanistan,* p. 68.

91. *Ibid.,* p. 65.

92. *Ibid.,* p. 78.

93. See "How to Make a Killing in Kabul: Western Security and a Crisis in Afghanistan," *Mail* (UK) online, February 28, 2011, available from *www.dailymail.co.uk/home/moslive/article-1360216/ How-make-killing-Kabul-Western-security-crisis-Afghanistan.html.*

94. *Inquiry into the Role and Oversight of Private Security Contractors in Afghanistan,* p. ii.

95. *Ibid.*

96. *Ibid.*

97. *Ibid.*

98. *Ibid.,* p. iii.

99. *Ibid.,* p. iv.

100. Rep. John F. Tierney, Chair, Subcommittee on National Security and Foreign Affairs, Committee on Oversight and Gov-

ernment Reform, U.S. House of Representatives, *Warlord Inc.: Extortion and Corruption along the U.S. Supply Chain in Afghanistan,* Washington, DC: U.S. House of Representatives, 2010.

101. *Ibid.*, p. 1.

102. *Ibid.*, p. 3.

103. *Ibid.*

104. For a discussion of shadow governance, see Thomas R. Mockaitis, *Resolving Insurgencies,* Carlisle, PA: Strategic Studies Institute, U.S. Army War College, 2011, pp. 10-11.

105. *Ibid.*, pp. 76-77.

106. *Warlord Inc.*, p. 48.

107. Karl Forsberg and Kimberly Kagan, "Consolidating Private Security Companies in Southern Afghanistan," Washington, DC: Institute for the Study of War, 2010, p. 1.

108. Sebastian Abbot, "Reckless Private Security Companies Anger Afghans," *Huffington Post* online, April 30, 2010, available from *www.huffingtonpost.com/huff-wires/20100430/as-afghan-security-contractors/.*

109. Quoted in Haseeb Humayoon, "President Hamid Karzai's Second Inaugural Address: Critical Points and Policy Implications," Washington, DC: Institute for the Study of War, 2009, p. 2.

110. *Ibid.*

111. *Ibid.*

112. *Ibid.*

113. *Ibid.*

114. *Ibid.*, p. vi.

115. *Ibid.*, p. vii.

116. Quoted in Cotton *et al.*, p. 27.

117. Ryan Kelly, "Citizen Soldiers and Civilian Contractors: Soldiers' Unit Cohesion and Retention Attitudes in the Total Force," *Journal of Political and Military Sociology*, Vol. 37, No. 2, Winter 2009, pp.133-159.

118. Cotton *et al.*, p. 21.

119. *Ibid.*

120. P. W. Singer, "Can't Win With 'Em, Can't Go To War Without 'Em: Private Military Contractors and Counterinsurgency," *Policy Paper* No. 4, Washington, DC: Brookings Institute, September 2007, p. 5.

121. Tiefer, p. 209.

122. Huma T. Yasin, "Playing Catch-up: Proposing the Creating of Status-Based Regulations to Bring Private Military Contractor Firms within the Purview of International and Domestic Law," *Emory International Law Review*, Vol. 25, Issue 1, 2011, p. 431.

123. *Ibid.*

124. Mayer, p. 397.

125. See Thomas R. Mockaitis, *Avoiding the Slippery Slope: Conducting Effective Interventions*, Carlisle, PA: Strategic Studies Institute, 2013.

126. Singer, "Can't Win With 'Em, Can't Go to War Without 'Em," p. 5.

127. John Michaels, "Privatization's Pretensions," *University of Chicago Law Review*, Vol. 77, 2010, p. 717.

128. *Ibid.*, pp. 721-722.